9/13

Barack Obama's Family Tree
Roots of Achievement

Amelie von Zumbusch

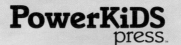

PowerKiDS press.

New York

Published in 2010 by The Rosen Publishing Group, Inc.
29 East 21st Street, New York, NY 10010

First Edition

Editors: Nicole Pristash and Maggie Murphy
Book Design: Kate Laczynski
Photo Researcher: Jessica Gerweck

Photo Credits: Cover, pp. 1, 6 (Abongo Obama, Auma Obama, Abo Obama, Bernard Obama, Kezia Obama) 18 Peter Macdiarmid/Getty Images; p. 4 Chuck Kennedy-Pool/Getty Images; p. 6 (Habiba Akumu Obama) Wikimedia Commons; pp. 6 (Sarah Onyango Obama), 20 © Jacob Wire/Rapport Press/Newscom; p. 6 (Mark Ndesandjo) ChinaFotoPress/Getty Images; pp. 7 (Stanley Dunham, Madelyn Payne Dunham), 10, 12 © AP Photo/Dunham Family Archives; pp. 7 (Barack Hussein Obama, Ann Dunham Soetoro, Lolo Soetoro), 8 (inset), 10 (inset), 14, 16 © Rapport/Newscom; p. 7 (Barack Obama, Michelle Obama) Pascal Le Segretain/Getty Images; p. 7 (Maya Soetoro-Ng, Malia Obama) Chip Somodevilla/Getty Images; p. 7 (Sasha Obama) Kent Nishimura-Pool/Getty Images; p. 8 Shutterstock; p. 14 Maxine Box/Getty Images; p. 14 © AP Photo/Obama Presidential Campaign.

Library of Congress Cataloging-in-Publication Data

Zumbusch, Amelie von.
  Barack Obama's family tree : roots of achievement / Amelie von Zumbusch. — 1st ed.
      p. cm. — (Making history: the Obamas)
  Includes index.
  ISBN 978-1-4358-9390-0 (library binding) — ISBN 978-1-4358-9872-1 (pbk.) — ISBN 978-1-4358-9873-8 (6-pack)
  1. Obama, Barack—Family—Juvenile literature. 2. Presidents—United States—Family—Juvenile literature. I. Title.
  E909.Z86 2010
  973.932092—dc22

                                    2009035759

Manufactured in the United States of America

CPSIA Compliance Information: Batch #WW10PK: For Further Information contact Rosen Publishing, New York, New York at 1-800-237-9932

Contents

A Strong Family

Being the president of the United States is a hard job. The president needs to have a strong sense of who he is. Today's president, Barack Obama, is our first African-American president. He draws strength from his **diverse** family. Obama's **relatives** live around the world. They belong to different races and faiths. Having relatives who are different from him has helped Obama understand other people's points of view.

People who are interested in family histories often draw charts called family trees. These show how everyone in a family is related. Obama's family tree is big and full of interesting people.

Here, Barack Obama stands next to his family as he is sworn into office as president. His half sisters Maya and Auma came to see him sworn in as well.

Barack Obama's Family Tree

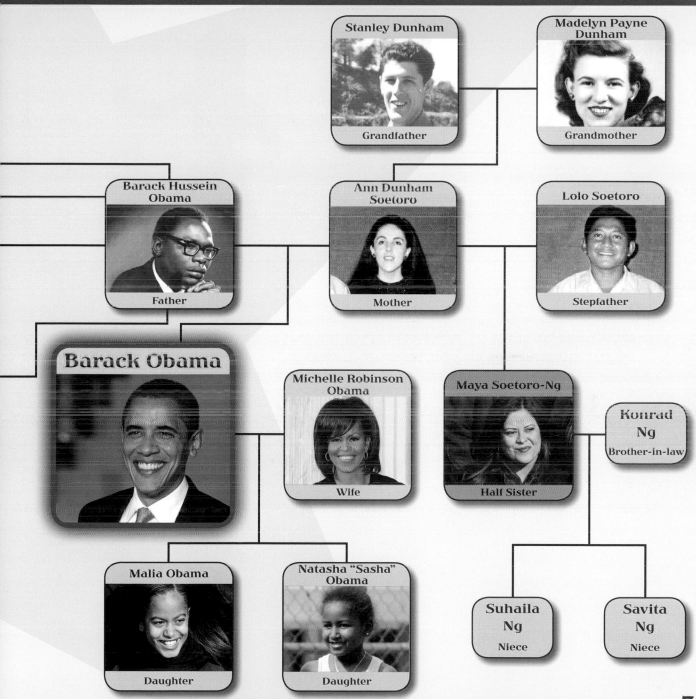

Stanley Dunham — Grandfather

Madelyn Payne Dunham — Grandmother

Barack Hussein Obama — Father

Ann Dunham Soetoro — Mother

Lolo Soetoro — Stepfather

Barack Obama

Michelle Robinson Obama — Wife

Maya Soetoro-Ng — Half Sister

Konrad Ng — Brother-in-law

Malia Obama — Daughter

Natasha "Sasha" Obama — Daughter

Suhaila Ng — Niece

Savita Ng — Niece

Born in Beautiful Hawaii

Barack Hussein Obama was born on August 4, 1961, in Hawaii. His mother was a white American student named Stanley Ann Dunham. People called her Ann. His father, Barack Hussein Obama Sr., was a black student from Kenya. At that time, many people thought white people and black people should not be allowed to marry each other. However, young Barack's parents had great hope for his **future**.

While his son was still a baby, the older Barack moved to Massachusetts to continue his studies. In 1964, Barack and Ann **divorced**. Ann's parents, Madelyn and Stanley Dunham, helped Ann raise young Barack in Hawaii.

Obama was born in Honolulu, the capital of Hawaii, shown here. *Inset:* Young Obama plays in the ocean.

A Lively Grandfather

Barack Obama's grandfather Stanley Dunham played a big part in his life. Dunham grew up in Wichita, Kansas. He was talkative and had a sharp sense of humor. As a young man, Dunham traveled across the country looking for work and fun.

After returning to Kansas, he fell in love with a quiet young woman named Madelyn Payne. The pair got married in 1940. Soon after their wedding, the United States entered **World War II**. Dunham joined the military to fight for his country. The Dunhams' daughter, Ann, was born during the war. After the war, Dunham worked as a salesman.

Top Left: Dunham as a soldier in the U.S. Army in 1944. *Top Right:* Dunham with Ann in 1946. *Bottom:* Dunham and young Obama in 1961.

A Practical Grandmother

During World War II, Barack Obama's grandmother Madelyn Dunham worked in a plant that made military planes. After the war, Stanley Dunham's dreams of a better life pushed the family from state to state. They lived in Kansas, California, Texas, and Washington before settling in Hawaii.

While her husband was a dreamer, Madelyn Dunham was more **practical**. She believed in hard work. In Hawaii, she took a job in a bank. In time, she worked her way up to become the bank's first female vice president. Obama has said that he owes his practicality and hardworking ways to his grandmother.

Obama called his grandmother Toot. This name was short for *tutu*, which is a Hawaiian word for "grandmother."

Smart with a Kind Heart

Stanley Ann Dunham was born in Wichita, Kansas, on November 29, 1942. She was smart and wanted to know more about the world. Her interest in other **cultures** was one thing that drew her to Barack Obama Sr. Although their marriage did not last, she tried to teach young Barack about his **heritage**.

In time, Ann married an Indonesian student named Lolo Soetoro. In 1967, the family moved to Indonesia. Barack's half sister Maya was born there. After that marriage ended, Ann returned to Hawaii to study **anthropology**. She then traveled to many different countries around the world.

Top Left: Ann's 1958 high school picture. *Top Right:* Ann with Obama in the 1960s. *Bottom:* Ann with Lolo Soetoro (left), Maya (center), and Obama.

Roots in Kenya

Young Barack Obama saw little of his father. They spent just one month together after his parents divorced. However, his mother told Obama many stories about how smart his father was. Obama tried hard to live up to his example.

Barack Obama Sr. was born in 1936, in Alego, Kenya. His parents were Akumu and Hussein Onyango Obama. He was a member of the Luo tribe. Barack was smart and did well in school. He won a **scholarship** to study in the United States. There, he studied **economics**. He hoped to use what he had learned to help Kenya.

Growing up in Kenya, Barack Obama Sr., shown here, herded goats with his father. *Inset:* Obama Sr. with Ann Dunham in Honolulu.

The Father of Eight Children

When his son Barack was still young, Barack Obama Sr. returned to Kenya. He worked as an economist for the Kenyan government. However, he got into trouble for speaking out about the government's problems.

Before coming to the United States, Obama had been married to a woman named Kezia. They had a son named Abongo and a daughter named Auma. Abongo is also called either Roy or Malik. After Obama divorced Ann Dunham, he married a woman named Ruth. They had two sons, Mark and David. Kezia also had two more sons, Abo and Bernard. His youngest son, George, was from another relationship.

Here, Obama is shown with some of his Kenyan relatives. Among them are Abongo, Abo, Bernard, Auma, and Kezia.

Visiting Kenya

Barack Obama Sr. died in 1982, while his son Barack was in **college**. Obama was sad that he did not get to know his father. However, in the 1980s, Obama met his half brother Roy, who was visiting the United States. His half sister Auma came to visit him, too. They both pushed him to go to Kenya and meet his relatives.

In 1988, Barack visited Kenya for several weeks. He met many relatives, including half brothers, uncles, aunts, cousins, and his stepgrandmother Sarah. Obama later wrote that the visit helped bring together "my outward self with my inward self in an important way."

Here, Obama carries a bag of vegetables for his stepgrandmother Sarah (right) during a visit to Kenya.

The Obamas' Future

As the years have passed, Barack Obama's family tree has grown. In 1992, he married Michelle Robinson. Their daughter Malia was born in 1998. Another daughter, named Sasha, followed in 2001.

When Obama was **elected** the country's first African-American president, many Americans were proud. His win proved that many Americans valued the country's diverse makeup. Barack Obama's family clearly shows that diversity. It includes whites, blacks, and Asians. While the president is Christian, several of his relatives are Muslim or Buddhist. As Obama said on the day he became president, "our patchwork heritage is a strength, not a weakness."

Glossary

anthropology (an-thruh-PAH-luh-jee) The study of human behavior, beliefs, and society.

college (KO-lij) A school one can go to after high school.

cultures (KUL-churz) The beliefs, practices, and arts of groups of people.

diverse (dy-VERS) Different.

divorced (dih-VORSD) Ended a marriage legally.

economics (eh-kuh-NAH-miks) The study of production and supply and demands of goods and services.

elected (ee-LEK-tid) Picked for an office by voters.

future (FYOO-chur) The time that is coming.

heritage (HER-uh-tij) The stories and ways of doing things that are handed down from parent to child.

practical (PRAK-tih-kul) Interested in real-world answers to problems.

relatives (REH-luh-tivz) Kin, or people in the same family who share the same blood.

scholarship (SKAH-lur-ship) Money given to someone to pay for school.

World War II (WURLD WOR TOO) A war fought by the United States, Great Britain, France, and the Soviet Union against Germany, Japan, and Italy from 1939 to 1945.

Index

Web Sites

Due to the changing nature of Internet links, PowerKids Press has developed an online list of Web sites related to the subject of this book. This site is updated regularly. Please use this link to access the list:
www.powerkidslinks.com/obamas/tree/